Machines and Motion

Wheels and Axles

by Kirsten Chang

Bullfrog Books

Ideas for Parents and Teachers

Bullfrog Books let children practice reading informational text at the earliest reading levels. Repetition, familiar words, and photo labels support early readers.

Before Reading

- Discuss the cover photo. What does it tell them?

- Look at the picture glossary together. Read and discuss the words.

Read the Book

- "Walk" through the book and look at the photos. Let the child ask questions. Point out the photo labels.

- Read the book to the child, or have him or her read independently.

After Reading

- Prompt the child to think more. Ask: Wheels and axles are everywhere. Where do you see them? What do they help you accomplish?

Bullfrog Books are published by Jump!
5357 Penn Avenue South
Minneapolis, MN 55419
www.jumplibrary.com

Library of Congress Cataloging-in-Publication Data

Names: Chang, Kirsten, author.
Title: Wheels and axles / by Kirsten Chang.
Description: Minneapolis, MN : Jump!, Inc., [2018]
Series: Machines and motions
"Bullfrog Books are published by Jump!"
Audience: Ages 5–8. | Audience: K to grade 3.
Includes bibliographical references and index.
Identifiers: LCCN 2017049613 (print)
LCCN 2017048255 (ebook)
ISBN 9781624968655 (ebook)
ISBN 9781624968631 (hardcover : alk. paper)
ISBN 9781624968648 (pbk.)
Subjects: LCSH: Wheels—Juvenile literature.
Axles—Juvenile literature.
Simple machines—Juvenile literature.
Classification: LCC TJ181.5 (print)
LCC TJ181.5 .C43 2018 (ebook) | DDC 621.8/11—dc23
LC record available at https://lccn.loc.gov/2017049613

Editor: Kristine Spanier
Book Designer: Molly Ballanger

Photo Credits: Oleksandr Grechin/Shutterstock, cover; igorstevanovic/Shutterstock, 1; ericlefrancais/Shutterstock, 3; Sergey Novikov/Shutterstock, 4, 5, 23br; Maksim Toome/Shutterstock, 6–7; lzf/Shutterstock, 8–9, 23tl; kali9/iStock, 10–11, 23tr; ANURAK PONGPATIMET/Shutterstock, 12 (child); Pixavril/Shutterstock, 12 (toys); Mike Flippo/Shutterstock, 13 (wagon); Dimitar Sotirov/Shutterstock, 13 (toys); Ariel Skelley/Shutterstock, 14–15; Mint Images/Alamy, 16; trekandshoot/Shutterstock, 17, 23bl; Vladislav Gajic/Shutterstock, 18–19; Wavebreakmedia/iStock, 20–21; kurhan/Shutterstock, 24.

Printed in the United States of America at Corporate Graphics in North Mankato, Minnesota.

Table of Contents

Get Moving

What is a wheel and axle?

It is a simple machine.

It only has two parts.

wheel

axle

The wheel turns.

7

7

axle

The axle keeps the wheel in place.

It stops the wheel from rolling away!

Wheels and axles make moving things easier.

axle

Sam needs to move her toys.

A wagon helps.

Jan needs to move
some flowers.

A wheelbarrow helps.

wheelbarrow

Wheels and axles move a car.

They move a load.

load

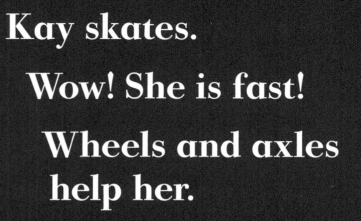

Kay skates.

Wow! She is fast!

Wheels and axles help her.

Need to move?

Wheels and axles
can help!

Build a Wheel and Axle

Wheels and axles help a car move. Build a clothespin car with working wheels and axles. Have an adult help you with this simple activity.

You will need:

- clothespin
- straw
- two twist ties
- four same-sized buttons
- scissors
- glue

Directions:

❶ Insert one of the twist ties into a hole in one of the buttons.

❷ Thread about an inch of the twist tie through a second hole and back through the other side of the button.

❸ Tightly twist the two pieces at the back of the button together.

❹ Cut two 1-inch pieces from the straw. Put the twist tie through one of the straw pieces.

❺ Thread the open end of the twist tie through the second button, then thread it back through the second hole. Twist it together.

❻ Repeat steps one through five for the second pair of buttons.

❼ Open the clothespin and place the straw from one set of wheels in the hole of the clothespin opening. Close the clothespin. The twist tie needs to be able to turn freely inside the straw.

❽ Add a dot of white glue to the back of the clothespin near the spring.

❾ Push the second set of wheels toward the spring into the glue. Wait a minute or two for it to dry.

❿ Take your clothespin car for a spin!

Picture Glossary

axle
A bar on which
a wheel turns.

simple machine
A tool used to make
work easier, such as
an inclined plane, lever,
pulley, screw, wedge,
or wheel and axle.

load
The weight
being lifted
or moved.

wheel
A round object
that turns
on an axle.

Index

To Learn More

Learning more is as easy as 1, 2, 3.

1) Go to www.factsurfer.com

2) Enter "wheelsandaxles" into the search box.

3) Click the "Surf" button to see a list of websites.

With factsurfer.com, finding more information is just a click away.

24